Apple Cider Donut Recipes

Delightful Creations for Apple Lovers

While every precaution has been taken in the preparation of this book, the publisher assumes no responsibility for errors or omissions, or for damages resulting from the use of the information contained herein.

APPLE CIDER DONUT RECIPES

First edition. December 10, 2023.

ISBN: 979-8223089025

Written by Jose Maria.

Table of Contents

Jose Maria

Chapter 1: Classic Apple Cider Donuts

Apple cider donuts, a timeless classic, have been a beloved treat for generations. These soft, moist, and slightly tangy delights are the perfect way to welcome the fall season. In this chapter, we'll explore the essence of the classic apple cider donut and learn how to make them in your own kitchen. Whether you prefer them dusted with cinnamon sugar or glazed to perfection, these recipes will satisfy your cravings and bring the cozy aroma of autumn into your home.

Recipe 1: Traditional Cinnamon-Sugar Donuts
Ingredients:

- 2 cups all-purpose flour
- 1/2 cup granulated sugar
- 2 tsp baking powder
- 1/2 tsp baking soda
- 1/2 tsp salt
- 1 tsp ground cinnamon
- 1/2 tsp ground nutmeg
- 1/2 cup apple cider
- 1/4 cup buttermilk
- 2 large eggs
- 2 tbsp unsalted butter, melted
- 1 tsp vanilla extract
- Vegetable oil for frying

For the Coating:

- 1/2 cup granulated sugar
- 1 tsp ground cinnamon

Instructions:

1. In a mixing bowl, whisk together the flour, granulated sugar, baking powder, baking soda, salt, cinnamon, and nutmeg.
2. In another bowl, combine the apple cider, buttermilk, eggs, melted butter, and vanilla extract.
3. Pour the wet ingredients into the dry ingredients and stir until just combined. Be careful not to overmix; a few lumps are okay.
4. Heat about 2 inches of vegetable oil in a deep, heavy-bottomed pot to 350°F (175°C). Use a candy thermometer to ensure accuracy.
5. While the oil is heating, prepare a plate lined with paper towels and a separate shallow bowl with the coating mixture (sugar and cinnamon).
6. Once the oil is hot, carefully drop spoonfuls of the dough into the hot oil, being cautious not to overcrowd the pot. Fry for about 2-3 minutes per side, or until the donuts are golden brown.
7. Remove the donuts from the oil using a slotted spoon and place them on the paper towel-lined plate to drain briefly.
8. While the donuts are still warm, roll them in the sugar-cinnamon mixture until they're evenly coated.
9. Serve the donuts warm and enjoy the classic taste of apple cider goodness!

Recipe 2: Glazed Apple Cider Delights
Ingredients:

- 2 cups apple cider
- 2 cups all-purpose flour
- 1/2 cup whole wheat flour
- 1/2 cup granulated sugar
- 1 tsp baking powder
- 1/2 tsp baking soda
- 1/2 tsp salt

- 1/2 tsp ground cinnamon
- 1/4 tsp ground nutmeg
- 1/4 tsp ground cloves
- 1/4 cup unsalted butter, softened
- 2 large eggs
- 1 tsp vanilla extract

For the Glaze:

- 2 cups powdered sugar
- 1/4 cup apple cider
- 1 tsp vanilla extract

Instructions:

1. In a saucepan, bring the apple cider to a boil over medium-high heat. Reduce the heat and simmer for about 15-20 minutes or until the cider has reduced to about 1/2 cup. Allow it to cool.
2. In a mixing bowl, combine the all-purpose flour, whole wheat flour, granulated sugar, baking powder, baking soda, salt, cinnamon, nutmeg, and cloves.
3. In another bowl, cream together the softened butter, eggs, and vanilla extract.
4. Stir the reduced apple cider into the wet ingredients.
5. Gradually add the dry ingredients to the wet mixture, mixing until just combined.
6. Cover the dough and chill it in the refrigerator for at least 1 hour.
7. Preheat your oven to 375°F (190°C) and grease a donut pan.
8. Spoon the chilled dough into the prepared donut pan, filling each mold about 2/3 full.
9. Bake for 12-15 minutes or until the donuts are lightly golden and spring back when touched.

10. While the donuts are cooling, prepare the glaze by whisking together the powdered sugar, apple cider, and vanilla extract until smooth.
11. Dip each cooled donut into the glaze, allowing any excess to drip off.
12. Place the glazed donuts on a wire rack to set.
13. Serve these heavenly glazed apple cider donuts to friends and family, and watch them disappear!

Classic apple cider donuts are a true testament to the magic of fall. Whether you savor the simplicity of cinnamon-sugar-coated donuts or prefer the sweet and tangy allure of glazed delights, these recipes capture the essence of autumn in every bite. Feel free to get creative with your decorations or enjoy them as they are—a taste of tradition that never goes out of style.

Chapter 2: Seasonal Variations

As the seasons change, so do our cravings. In this chapter, we'll explore delightful variations of the classic apple cider donut that embrace the flavors and ingredients of each season. From the cozy warmth of pumpkin spice to the bright tang of cranberry-apple and the sweet allure of maple-glazed treats, these recipes will keep your taste buds dancing all year round.

Recipe 1: Pumpkin Spice Apple Cider Donuts
Ingredients:

- 2 cups all-purpose flour
- 1/2 cup granulated sugar
- 1 tsp baking powder
- 1/2 tsp baking soda
- 1/2 tsp salt
- 1 tsp ground cinnamon
- 1/2 tsp ground nutmeg
- 1/4 tsp ground cloves
- 1/2 cup apple cider
- 1/2 cup canned pumpkin puree
- 2 large eggs
- 2 tbsp unsalted butter, melted
- 1 tsp vanilla extract

For the Coating:

- 1/2 cup granulated sugar
- 1 tsp ground cinnamon
- 1/4 tsp ground nutmeg

Instructions:

1. In a mixing bowl, whisk together the flour, granulated sugar, baking powder, baking soda, salt, cinnamon, nutmeg, and cloves.
2. In another bowl, combine the apple cider, pumpkin puree, eggs, melted butter, and vanilla extract.
3. Pour the wet ingredients into the dry ingredients and stir until just combined. Avoid overmixing.
4. Preheat your oven to 350°F (175°C) and grease a donut pan.
5. Spoon the batter into the donut molds, filling each about 2/3 full.
6. Bake for 15-18 minutes or until a toothpick inserted into a donut comes out clean.
7. While the donuts are still warm, combine the sugar, cinnamon, and nutmeg in a shallow bowl. Roll the donuts in this mixture until evenly coated.

Enjoy the cozy flavors of fall with these pumpkin spice apple cider donuts!

Recipe 2: Cranberry-Apple Bliss
Ingredients:

- 2 cups all-purpose flour
- 1/2 cup granulated sugar
- 1 tsp baking powder
- 1/2 tsp baking soda
- 1/2 tsp salt
- 1/2 tsp ground cinnamon
- 1/4 tsp ground nutmeg
- 1/2 cup apple cider
- 1/2 cup unsweetened applesauce
- 2 large eggs
- 2 tbsp unsalted butter, melted
- 1 tsp vanilla extract

- 1 cup fresh or frozen cranberries, chopped

For the Glaze:

- 1 cup powdered sugar
- 2-3 tbsp apple cider

Instructions:

1. In a mixing bowl, whisk together the flour, granulated sugar, baking powder, baking soda, salt, cinnamon, and nutmeg.
2. In another bowl, combine the apple cider, applesauce, eggs, melted butter, and vanilla extract.
3. Pour the wet ingredients into the dry ingredients and stir until just combined. Do not overmix.
4. Gently fold in the chopped cranberries.
5. Preheat your oven to 350°F (175°C) and grease a donut pan.
6. Spoon the batter into the donut molds, filling each about 2/3 full.
7. Bake for 15-18 minutes or until a toothpick inserted into a donut comes out clean.
8. Allow the donuts to cool slightly in the pan before transferring them to a wire rack.
9. In a small bowl, whisk together the powdered sugar and apple cider to make the glaze. Drizzle the glaze over the cooled donuts.
10. Savor the harmonious blend of cranberries and apples in these delightful cranberry-apple donuts.

Recipe 3: Maple-Glazed Fall Favorites
Ingredients:

- 2 cups all-purpose flour
- 1/2 cup granulated sugar
- 1 tsp baking powder
- 1/2 tsp baking soda
- 1/2 tsp salt
- 1/2 tsp ground cinnamon
- 1/4 tsp ground nutmeg
- 1/2 cup apple cider
- 1/4 cup pure maple syrup
- 2 large eggs
- 2 tbsp unsalted butter, melted
- 1 tsp vanilla extract

For the Glaze:

- 1 cup powdered sugar
- 2-3 tbsp pure maple syrup

Instructions:

1. In a mixing bowl, whisk together the flour, granulated sugar, baking powder, baking soda, salt, cinnamon, and nutmeg.
2. In another bowl, combine the apple cider, pure maple syrup, eggs, melted butter, and vanilla extract.
3. Pour the wet ingredients into the dry ingredients and stir until just combined. Be careful not to overmix.
4. Preheat your oven to 350°F (175°C) and grease a donut pan.
5. Spoon the batter into the donut molds, filling each about 2/3 full.
6. Bake for 15-18 minutes or until a toothpick inserted into a donut comes out clean.
7. Allow the donuts to cool slightly in the pan before transferring them to a wire rack.

8. In a small bowl, whisk together the powdered sugar and pure maple syrup to make the glaze. Drizzle the glaze over the cooled donuts.

These maple-glazed fall favorites are the perfect indulgence on crisp autumn days.

Chapter 3: Creative Twists

While classic apple cider donuts are a timeless delight, sometimes it's fun to get creative and put a unique spin on this beloved treat. In this chapter, we'll explore three inventive ways to enjoy the flavors of apple cider donuts: as muffins, in a comforting bread pudding, and transformed into delightful ice cream sandwiches. These recipes will take your apple cider donut experience to a whole new level of deliciousness.

Recipe 1: Apple Cider Donut Muffins

Ingredients:

- 2 cups all-purpose flour
- 1/2 cup granulated sugar
- 2 tsp baking powder
- 1/2 tsp baking soda
- 1/2 tsp salt
- 1 tsp ground cinnamon
- 1/2 tsp ground nutmeg
- 1/2 cup apple cider
- 1/4 cup buttermilk
- 2 large eggs
- 2 tbsp unsalted butter, melted
- 1 tsp vanilla extract

For the Topping:

- 1/4 cup granulated sugar
- 1/2 tsp ground cinnamon
- 2 tbsp unsalted butter, melted

Instructions:

1. Preheat your oven to 375°F (190°C) and line a muffin tin with

paper liners or grease it.

2. In a mixing bowl, whisk together the flour, granulated sugar, baking powder, baking soda, salt, cinnamon, and nutmeg.
3. In another bowl, combine the apple cider, buttermilk, eggs, melted butter, and vanilla extract.
4. Pour the wet ingredients into the dry ingredients and stir until just combined. Do not overmix.
5. Spoon the batter into the muffin cups, filling each about 2/3 full.
6. Bake for 18-20 minutes or until a toothpick inserted into a muffin comes out clean.
7. While the muffins are still warm, prepare the topping by mixing the sugar and cinnamon in one bowl and melting the butter in another.
8. Dip the top of each muffin into the melted butter and then into the sugar-cinnamon mixture to coat.

Enjoy these muffin-sized apple cider donuts with a twist!

Recipe 2: Apple Cider Donut Bread Pudding

Ingredients:

- 6 apple cider donuts, cut into bite-sized pieces
- 2 cups milk
- 1/2 cup heavy cream
- 3 large eggs
- 1/2 cup granulated sugar
- 1 tsp vanilla extract
- 1/2 tsp ground cinnamon
- 1/4 tsp ground nutmeg
- Pinch of salt
- Optional: Whipped cream and caramel sauce for serving

Instructions:

1. Preheat your oven to 350°F (175°C). Grease a baking dish.
2. Arrange the bite-sized apple cider donut pieces in the greased baking dish.
3. In a saucepan, heat the milk and heavy cream over medium heat until it's steaming but not boiling. Remove from heat.
4. In a separate bowl, whisk together the eggs, granulated sugar, vanilla extract, cinnamon, nutmeg, and a pinch of salt.
5. Gradually add the hot milk mixture to the egg mixture, whisking constantly.
6. Pour the custard mixture over the donut pieces in the baking dish, pressing the donuts down gently to ensure they absorb the liquid.
7. Allow the mixture to sit for about 15 minutes to ensure the donuts soak up the custard.
8. Bake for 35-40 minutes or until the top is golden brown and the pudding is set.
9. Serve warm, optionally topped with whipped cream and caramel sauce, for a comforting apple cider donut bread pudding experience.

Recipe 3: Donut Ice Cream Sandwiches
Ingredients:

- 6 apple cider donuts
- 1 pint of your favorite ice cream (e.g., vanilla, cinnamon, or caramel)
- Optional toppings (e.g., chopped nuts, chocolate chips, or caramel drizzle)

Instructions:

1. Slice the apple cider donuts in half horizontally to create a top and bottom for each sandwich.

2. Allow the ice cream to soften slightly at room temperature for easier scooping.
3. Place a scoop of ice cream onto the bottom half of a donut.
4. Top the ice cream with the other half of the donut to create a sandwich.
5. If desired, roll the edges of the sandwich in your choice of toppings.
6. Place the sandwiches in the freezer for at least 30 minutes to firm up.
7. Indulge in these donut ice cream sandwiches, a delightful fusion of warm and cold, crispy and creamy.

Chapter 4: Healthier Options

For those looking for a guilt-free indulgence or accommodating dietary restrictions, this chapter offers three healthier alternatives to classic apple cider donuts. Whether you prefer the heartiness of whole wheat, a lower sugar option, or vegan and gluten-free alternatives, these recipes prove that you can enjoy the delightful flavors of apple cider donuts while making healthier choices.

Recipe 1: Baked Apple Cider Donuts with Whole Wheat

Ingredients:

- 1 cup whole wheat flour
- 1 cup all-purpose flour
- 1/2 cup granulated sugar
- 2 tsp baking powder
- 1/2 tsp baking soda
- 1/2 tsp salt
- 1 tsp ground cinnamon
- 1/2 tsp ground nutmeg
- 1/2 cup apple cider
- 1/2 cup unsweetened applesauce
- 2 large eggs
- 2 tbsp unsalted butter, melted
- 1 tsp vanilla extract

Instructions:

1. Preheat your oven to 350°F (175°C) and grease a donut pan.
2. In a mixing bowl, whisk together the whole wheat flour, all-purpose flour, granulated sugar, baking powder, baking soda, salt, cinnamon, and nutmeg.
3. In another bowl, combine the apple cider, applesauce, eggs,

melted butter, and vanilla extract.

4. Pour the wet ingredients into the dry ingredients and stir until just combined. Be careful not to overmix.

5. Spoon the batter into the donut molds, filling each about 2/3 full.

6. Bake for 12-15 minutes or until a toothpick inserted into a donut comes out clean.

These baked whole wheat apple cider donuts are a healthier take on the classic treat.

Recipe 2: Low-Sugar Apple Cider Donuts
Ingredients:

- 2 cups all-purpose flour
- 1/4 cup granulated sugar
- 2 tsp baking powder
- 1/2 tsp baking soda
- 1/2 tsp salt
- 1 tsp ground cinnamon
- 1/2 tsp ground nutmeg
- 1/2 cup apple cider
- 1/4 cup unsweetened applesauce
- 2 large eggs
- 2 tbsp unsalted butter, melted
- 1 tsp vanilla extract

For the Coating:

- 2 tbsp granulated sugar
- 1/2 tsp ground cinnamon

Instructions:

1. In a mixing bowl, whisk together the flour, granulated sugar, baking powder, baking soda, salt, cinnamon, and nutmeg.
2. In another bowl, combine the apple cider, applesauce, eggs, melted butter, and vanilla extract.
3. Pour the wet ingredients into the dry ingredients and stir until just combined. Avoid overmixing.
4. Preheat your oven to 350°F (175°C) and grease a donut pan.
5. Spoon the batter into the donut molds, filling each about 2/3 full.
6. Bake for 12-15 minutes or until a toothpick inserted into a donut comes out clean.
7. While the donuts are still warm, combine the sugar and cinnamon in a shallow bowl. Roll the donuts in this mixture to coat.

These low-sugar apple cider donuts offer a sweet treat with reduced sugar content.

Recipe 3: Vegan and Gluten-Free Alternatives
Ingredients:

- 1 1/2 cups gluten-free all-purpose flour
- 1/2 cup almond flour
- 1/2 cup coconut sugar
- 2 tsp baking powder
- 1/2 tsp baking soda
- 1/2 tsp salt
- 1 tsp ground cinnamon
- 1/2 tsp ground nutmeg
- 1/2 cup unsweetened applesauce
- 1/2 cup apple cider
- 1/4 cup coconut oil, melted (or vegetable oil for a nut-free option)
- 1 tsp vanilla extract

Instructions:

1. Preheat your oven to 350°F (175°C) and grease a donut pan.
2. In a mixing bowl, whisk together the gluten-free all-purpose flour, almond flour, coconut sugar, baking powder, baking soda, salt, cinnamon, and nutmeg.
3. In another bowl, combine the applesauce, apple cider, melted coconut oil (or vegetable oil), and vanilla extract.
4. Pour the wet ingredients into the dry ingredients and stir until just combined. Do not overmix.
5. Spoon the batter into the donut molds, filling each about 2/3 full.
6. Bake for 12-15 minutes or until a toothpick inserted into a donut comes out clean.

These vegan and gluten-free apple cider donuts are perfect for those with dietary restrictions.

Chapter 5: International Flavors

Apple cider donuts have captured the hearts of people worldwide, and each culture has its unique take on this beloved treat. In this chapter, we'll embark on a culinary journey to explore international flavors inspired by apple cider donuts. From the French-inspired "Pommes au Cidre Beignets" to the German "Apfelwein Donuts" and the delightful "Japanese Apple Cider Donuts," these recipes will introduce you to a world of apple-infused delights.

Recipe 1: French-inspired Pommes au Cidre Beignets
Ingredients:

- 2 cups all-purpose flour
- 1/4 cup granulated sugar
- 2 tsp baking powder
- 1/2 tsp salt
- 1/2 cup apple cider
- 2 large eggs
- 2 tbsp unsalted butter, melted
- 1 tsp vanilla extract
- 2 cups vegetable oil for frying
- Powdered sugar for dusting

Instructions:

1. In a mixing bowl, whisk together the flour, granulated sugar, baking powder, and salt.
2. In another bowl, combine the apple cider, eggs, melted butter, and vanilla extract.
3. Pour the wet ingredients into the dry ingredients and stir until just combined. Avoid overmixing.
4. Heat the vegetable oil in a deep pot or frying pan to 350°F

(175°C).

5. Drop spoonfuls of the dough into the hot oil, frying until they are golden brown and puffed up, about 2-3 minutes per side.

6. Remove the beignets from the oil with a slotted spoon and drain them on paper towels.

Dust the warm beignets generously with powdered sugar and serve these French-inspired "Pommes au Cidre Beignets."

Recipe 2: German Apfelwein Donuts

Ingredients:

- 2 cups all-purpose flour
- 1/4 cup granulated sugar
- 2 tsp baking powder
- 1/2 tsp salt
- 1/2 cup apple cider
- 1/4 cup Apfelwein (German apple wine)
- 2 large eggs
- 2 tbsp unsalted butter, melted
- 1 tsp vanilla extract
- Vegetable oil for frying
- Powdered sugar for dusting

Instructions:

1. In a mixing bowl, whisk together the flour, granulated sugar, baking powder, and salt.

2. In another bowl, combine the apple cider, Apfelwein, eggs, melted butter, and vanilla extract.

3. Pour the wet ingredients into the dry ingredients and stir until just combined. Avoid overmixing.

4. Heat vegetable oil in a deep pot or frying pan to 350°F (175°C).

5. Drop spoonfuls of the dough into the hot oil, frying until they

are golden brown and puffed up, about 2-3 minutes per side.

6. Remove the donuts from the oil with a slotted spoon and drain them on paper towels.

Dust the warm donuts generously with powdered sugar and savor the German "Apfelwein Donuts."

Recipe 3: Japanese Apple Cider Donuts

Ingredients:

- 2 cups all-purpose flour
- 1/4 cup granulated sugar
- 2 tsp baking powder
- 1/2 tsp salt
- 1/2 cup apple cider
- 2 large eggs
- 2 tbsp unsalted butter, melted
- 1 tsp vanilla extract
- Vegetable oil for frying
- Matcha green tea powder and powdered sugar for dusting

Instructions:

1. In a mixing bowl, whisk together the flour, granulated sugar, baking powder, and salt.
2. In another bowl, combine the apple cider, eggs, melted butter, and vanilla extract.
3. Pour the wet ingredients into the dry ingredients and stir until just combined. Avoid overmixing.
4. Heat vegetable oil in a deep pot or frying pan to 350°F (175°C).
5. Drop spoonfuls of the dough into the hot oil, frying until they are golden brown and puffed up, about 2-3 minutes per side.
6. Remove the donuts from the oil with a slotted spoon and drain them on paper towels.

Dust the warm donuts with a mixture of matcha green tea powder and powdered sugar to create the delightful "Japanese Apple Cider Donuts."

Chapter 6: Mini Donuts and Donut Holes

Sometimes, the best things come in small packages. In this chapter, we'll dive into the world of mini apple cider donuts and delightful donut holes. These bite-sized treats are perfect for snacking, sharing, or indulging in a guilt-free mini-dessert. We'll also explore a variety of creative dipping sauces to elevate your mini donut and donut hole experience.

Recipe 1: Mini Apple Cider Donuts

Ingredients:

- 1 cup all-purpose flour
- 1/4 cup granulated sugar
- 1 tsp baking powder
- 1/4 tsp baking soda
- 1/4 tsp salt
- 1/2 tsp ground cinnamon
- 1/4 tsp ground nutmeg
- 1/2 cup apple cider
- 1/4 cup buttermilk
- 1 large egg
- 1 tbsp unsalted butter, melted
- Vegetable oil for frying

For the Coating:

- 1/2 cup granulated sugar
- 1 tsp ground cinnamon

Instructions:

1. In a mixing bowl, whisk together the flour, granulated sugar, baking powder, baking soda, salt, cinnamon, and nutmeg.

2. In another bowl, combine the apple cider, buttermilk, egg, melted butter, and vanilla extract.
3. Pour the wet ingredients into the dry ingredients and stir until just combined. Avoid overmixing.
4. Preheat your oven to 350°F (175°C) and grease a mini donut pan.
5. Spoon the batter into the mini donut molds, filling each about 2/3 full.
6. Bake for 10-12 minutes or until a toothpick inserted into a mini donut comes out clean.
7. While the mini donuts are still warm, roll them in the sugar-cinnamon mixture to coat.

Enjoy these adorable mini apple cider donuts!

Recipe 2: Donut Hole Delights

Ingredients:

- Donut holes (you can use the recipe above or store-bought)

For the Coating:

- 1/2 cup powdered sugar
- 1/2 tsp ground cinnamon

Optional Toppings:

- Chopped nuts, sprinkles, chocolate chips

Instructions:

1. Prepare the donut holes using your preferred method, whether it's homemade or store-bought.
2. While the donut holes are still warm, prepare the coating by mixing the powdered sugar and ground cinnamon in a bowl.

3. Roll the warm donut holes in the sugar-cinnamon mixture until evenly coated.
4. For added fun, you can dip them in melted chocolate or caramel sauce and sprinkle with your choice of toppings.

These donut hole delights are perfect for snacking and sharing.

Recipe 3: Creative Dipping Sauces

Dipping Sauce 1: Caramel Apple Dip

Ingredients:

- 1/2 cup caramel sauce
- 2 tbsp apple cider
- 1/2 tsp ground cinnamon

Instructions:

1. In a small saucepan, combine the caramel sauce, apple cider, and ground cinnamon.
2. Heat the mixture over low heat, stirring until well combined and warmed through.
3. Serve this caramel apple dip with your mini donuts and donut holes.

Dipping Sauce 2: Chocolate Ganache

Ingredients:

- 1/2 cup heavy cream
- 1/2 cup semisweet chocolate chips
- 1 tsp vanilla extract

Instructions:

1. In a saucepan, heat the heavy cream over medium heat until it starts to simmer. Remove from heat.

2. Add the chocolate chips and vanilla extract to the hot cream. Let it sit for a minute, then stir until smooth and glossy.
3. Dip your mini donuts and donut holes into this decadent chocolate ganache.

Dipping Sauce 3: Maple Cream Cheese Glaze
Ingredients:

- 4 oz cream cheese, softened
- 2 tbsp maple syrup
- 1/2 cup powdered sugar
- 1-2 tbsp milk (adjust for desired consistency)

Instructions:

1. In a mixing bowl, beat the softened cream cheese until smooth.
2. Add the maple syrup and powdered sugar, mixing until well combined.
3. If the glaze is too thick, add milk a little at a time until you reach your desired consistency.
4. Dip your mini donuts and donut holes into this luscious maple cream cheese glaze.

Chapter 7: Cider and Donut Pairings

Pairing apple cider donuts with complementary beverages can elevate your tasting experience. In this chapter, we'll explore the art of pairing these delectable treats with a variety of beverages. Discover how to create the perfect apple cider and donut tasting guide, enjoy refreshing cider donut cocktails, and learn to pair donuts with the warmth of tea and coffee for a delightful culinary adventure.

Section 1: Apple Cider and Donut Tasting Guide

When it comes to pairing apple cider donuts with apple cider, the possibilities are endless. Here's a simple guide to help you navigate the world of flavors and textures:

Classic Pairing: Pair traditional apple cider donuts with unfiltered apple cider. The natural sweetness and slight tartness of the cider complement the warm spices and sweetness of the donuts.

Spiced Twist: If you're enjoying spiced apple cider donuts, try them with a spiced apple cider for an extra burst of autumnal flavor.

Caramel Delights: For caramel glazed donuts, consider pairing them with a caramel apple cider for an indulgent caramel apple experience.

Sharp and Sweet: If you have tart apple cider donuts, balance their acidity with a sweeter, milder apple cider.

Section 2: Cider Donut Cocktail Recipes

Cider Donut Martini
   Ingredients:

- 2 oz apple cider
- 1 oz vanilla vodka
- 1 oz butterscotch schnapps
- Ice
- Crushed graham crackers (for rimming)
- Caramel sauce (for rimming and drizzling)
- Cinnamon sugar (for rimming)

Instructions:

1. Rim a martini glass with caramel sauce and dip it in crushed graham crackers mixed with cinnamon sugar.
2. In a cocktail shaker, combine the apple cider, vanilla vodka, butterscotch schnapps, and ice.
3. Shake vigorously and strain the mixture into the prepared martini glass.
4. Drizzle caramel sauce on top for a delicious caramel apple twist.

Cider Donut Old Fashioned
Ingredients:

- 2 oz bourbon
- 1/2 oz pure maple syrup
- 2 dashes Angostura bitters
- 1 dash orange bitters
- Ice
- Apple cider donut hole (for garnish)
- Orange peel (for garnish)

Instructions:

1. In a mixing glass, combine the bourbon, maple syrup, Angostura bitters, and orange bitters.
2. Fill the glass with ice and stir until well chilled.
3. Strain the mixture into a rocks glass filled with ice.
4. Garnish with an apple cider donut hole and a strip of orange peel.

Section 3: Pairing Donuts with Tea and Coffee

Earl Grey and Apple Cider Donuts: The citrusy notes of Earl Grey tea pair beautifully with the fruity flavors of apple cider donuts. The bergamot in the tea adds a delightful dimension.

Chai and Spiced Donuts: The warm spices in chai tea, such as cinnamon, cardamom, and cloves, complement spiced apple cider donuts perfectly.

Coffee and Glazed Donuts: A classic pairing, the bitterness of coffee balances the sweetness of glazed donuts, creating a harmonious breakfast or dessert combination.

Herbal Tea and Tart Donuts: For tart apple cider donuts, consider herbal teas like hibiscus or chamomile, which won't overpower the subtle tartness.

Chapter 8: Holiday Specials

Holidays are the perfect time to indulge in festive treats, and apple cider donuts are no exception. In this chapter, we'll explore holiday-themed apple cider donuts that will add a touch of magic to your celebrations. From Thanksgiving's warm and comforting donuts to Christmas spiced delights and New Year's Eve donut desserts, these recipes will make your holidays even more memorable.

Recipe 1: Thanksgiving Apple Cider Donuts
Ingredients:

- 2 cups all-purpose flour
- 1/2 cup granulated sugar
- 2 tsp baking powder
- 1/2 tsp baking soda
- 1/2 tsp salt
- 1 tsp ground cinnamon
- 1/2 tsp ground nutmeg
- 1/2 cup apple cider
- 1/2 cup unsweetened applesauce
- 2 large eggs
- 2 tbsp unsalted butter, melted
- 1 tsp vanilla extract

For the Coating

- 1/2 cup powdered sugar
- 1 tsp ground cinnamon

Instructions:

1. In a mixing bowl, whisk together the flour, granulated sugar, baking powder, baking soda, salt, cinnamon, and nutmeg.

2. In another bowl, combine the apple cider, applesauce, eggs, melted butter, and vanilla extract.
3. Pour the wet ingredients into the dry ingredients and stir until just combined. Avoid overmixing.
4. Preheat your oven to 350°F (175°C) and grease a donut pan.
5. Spoon the batter into the donut molds, filling each about 2/3 full.
6. Bake for 12-15 minutes or until a toothpick inserted into a donut comes out clean.
7. While the donuts are still warm, roll them in a mixture of powdered sugar and ground cinnamon to coat.

These Thanksgiving apple cider donuts will bring warmth and comfort to your holiday table.

Recipe 2: Christmas Spiced Cider Donuts
Ingredients:

- 2 cups all-purpose flour
- 1/2 cup granulated sugar
- 2 tsp baking powder
- 1/2 tsp baking soda
- 1/2 tsp salt
- 1 tsp ground cinnamon
- 1/2 tsp ground nutmeg
- 1/4 tsp ground cloves
- 1/2 cup apple cider
- 1/2 cup unsweetened applesauce
- 2 large eggs
- 2 tbsp unsalted butter, melted
- 1 tsp vanilla extract

For the Glaze:

- 1 cup powdered sugar
- 2-3 tbsp milk
- 1/2 tsp ground cinnamon
- Pinch of ground nutmeg
- Red and green sprinkles (for decoration)

Instructions:

1. In a mixing bowl, whisk together the flour, granulated sugar, baking powder, baking soda, salt, cinnamon, nutmeg, and cloves.
2. In another bowl, combine the apple cider, applesauce, eggs, melted butter, and vanilla extract.
3. Pour the wet ingredients into the dry ingredients and stir until just combined. Avoid overmixing.
4. Preheat your oven to 350°F (175°C) and grease a donut pan.
5. Spoon the batter into the donut molds, filling each about 2/3 full.
6. Bake for 12-15 minutes or until a toothpick inserted into a donut comes out clean.
7. Allow the donuts to cool slightly in the pan before transferring them to a wire rack.
8. In a bowl, whisk together powdered sugar, milk, cinnamon, and nutmeg to make the glaze. Dip the cooled donuts into the glaze and decorate with red and green sprinkles for a festive touch.

These Christmas spiced cider donuts will add holiday cheer to your dessert table.

Recipe 3: New Year's Eve Donut Desserts
Ingredients:

- 6 apple cider donuts (any variety)
- 1 pint vanilla ice cream

- 1/2 cup caramel sauce
- 1/2 cup chocolate sauce
- Whipped cream
- Optional toppings: chopped nuts, sprinkles, maraschino cherries

Instructions:

1. Slice the apple cider donuts in half horizontally to create a top and bottom for each serving.
2. Place a scoop of vanilla ice cream onto the bottom half of each donut.
3. Drizzle caramel sauce over the ice cream.
4. Top with the other half of the donut to create a sandwich.
5. Drizzle chocolate sauce over the top of the donut sandwiches.
6. Add a dollop of whipped cream and any optional toppings you desire.

These New Year's Eve donut desserts are a sweet way to ring in the new year with style.

Chapter 9: DIY Apple Cider

There's something truly special about making your own apple cider from scratch. In this chapter, we'll guide you through the process of creating homemade apple cider, providing tips on using it in delicious donut recipes, and ensuring its proper storage and preservation for year-round enjoyment.

Section 1: Making Your Own Fresh Apple Cider

Ingredients:

- 12-15 apples (a mix of sweet and tart varieties)
- Water
- Optional: Cinnamon sticks, cloves, or star anise for added flavor

Instructions:

1. Wash and roughly chop the apples, including the cores and peels. Removing the seeds is important, but don't worry about perfection.
2. Place the chopped apples in a large stockpot and add enough water to cover them.
3. If desired, add cinnamon sticks, cloves, or star anise to infuse additional flavors.
4. Bring the mixture to a boil over medium-high heat. Once boiling, reduce the heat to a simmer and cover the pot.
5. Let it simmer for 1-2 hours, stirring occasionally. The apples should become soft and mushy.
6. Remove the pot from heat and allow it to cool slightly.
7. Strain the mixture through a fine-mesh sieve or cheesecloth into a large bowl or pitcher. Press down on the apple solids to extract as much liquid as possible.

Your homemade apple cider is ready! Serve it warm or chilled. If desired, sweeten with a bit of honey or sugar.

Section 2: Using Homemade Cider in Donut Recipes

Making donuts with homemade apple cider adds a fresh, natural sweetness and depth of flavor to your treats. Simply substitute the store-bought cider with your homemade version in any of your favorite donut recipes. You can use it in classic apple cider donuts, healthier versions, or international variations, such as the ones outlined in earlier chapters.

Section 3: Storing and Preserving Apple Cider

To ensure your homemade apple cider remains fresh and delicious:

Store it in the refrigerator in an airtight container. Homemade cider can typically be kept for up to 7-10 days.

If you want to extend its shelf life, consider freezing it in ice cube trays. Once frozen, transfer the cider cubes to a freezer bag. These can be used for cooking or making cider slushies.

If you wish to preserve your cider for an even longer period, consider canning it. Follow proper canning procedures to ensure safety and quality.

Tip: Before using refrigerated or frozen cider in recipes, thaw it in the refrigerator to avoid temperature shock.

Chapter 10: Apple Orchard Adventures

A visit to a local apple orchard is an enchanting experience that brings you closer to the source of your favorite fall treats. In this chapter, we'll explore the joys of visiting orchards, offer tips on selecting the best apples for cider and donuts, and provide delicious recipes inspired by apple cider donut food trucks you might encounter during your orchard adventures.

Section 1: Visiting Local Orchards

Exploring a local apple orchard is a delightful way to connect with nature and experience the beauty of autumn. Here are some tips for your orchard adventure:

Check the orchard's website or call ahead to confirm their hours and apple varieties available for picking.

Dress appropriately for the weather, wear comfortable shoes, and bring a hat and sunscreen.

Bring your own bags or baskets for apple picking, as some orchards may charge for bags.

Enjoy the scenic views, breathe in the crisp air, and consider taking a leisurely stroll through the orchard.

Support the orchard by purchasing fresh apples, cider, and other products they offer.

Section 2: Picking the Best Apples for Cider and Donuts

Selecting the right apples for cider and donuts is key to achieving the best flavors. Here are some apple varieties to consider:

For Cider:

Crispin: Known for its sweet, juicy flesh and mild tartness, Crispin apples make excellent cider with a balanced flavor.

Jonathan: These apples have a nice blend of sweet and tart flavors, making them ideal for cider.

Honeycrisp: While Honeycrisp apples are often enjoyed fresh, they can also contribute a sweet, honey-like flavor to cider.

For Donuts:

Granny Smith: Their tartness adds a delightful contrast to sweet donuts, especially when used in chunks or as a filling.

Cortland: These apples are slightly sweet and hold their shape well when baked, making them great for donut recipes.

Fuji: Sweet and crisp, Fuji apples work wonderfully in donuts, particularly when grated or finely chopped.

Section 3: Apple Cider Donut Food Truck Inspired Recipes

Get inspired by the delicious offerings of apple cider donut food trucks commonly found near orchards. Here are a few recipes inspired by these mobile delights:

Apple Cider Donut Ice Cream Sandwiches

Ingredients:

- Homemade or store-bought apple cider donuts
- Vanilla ice cream
- Caramel sauce
- Crushed graham crackers (optional)

Instructions:

1. Slice the apple cider donuts in half horizontally to create a top and bottom for each sandwich.
2. Place a scoop of vanilla ice cream onto the bottom half of each donut.
3. Drizzle caramel sauce over the ice cream.
4. Sandwich the ice cream with the top half of the donut.
5. Roll the sides of the ice cream in crushed graham crackers, if desired.

Apple Cider Donut Milkshake

Ingredients:

- 2 apple cider donuts
- 2 cups vanilla ice cream
- 1/2 cup apple cider
- 1/2 cup milk
- Whipped cream

- Cinnamon sugar (for garnish)

Instructions:

1. In a blender, combine the apple cider donuts, vanilla ice cream, apple cider, and milk.
2. Blend until smooth and creamy.
3. Pour the milkshake into glasses, top with whipped cream, and sprinkle with cinnamon sugar.

Apple Cider Donut Parfait
Ingredients:

- Apple cider donut holes
- Greek yogurt
- Apple slices
- Cinnamon
- Honey

Instructions:

1. Crumble apple cider donut holes into the bottom of a glass or bowl.
2. Layer with Greek yogurt, apple slices, and a sprinkle of cinnamon.
3. Drizzle honey over the top.

These recipes capture the spirit of apple orchard food trucks and are perfect for enjoying your freshly picked apples.

Chapter 11: Donut-Related Tools and Equipment

Having the right tools and equipment in your kitchen can make the process of creating perfect apple cider donuts a breeze. In this chapter, we'll explore the essential kitchen gadgets, guide you in choosing the right donut pans, and provide mixing and baking techniques to ensure your donuts turn out delicious every time.

Section 1: Essential Kitchen Gadgets

To craft mouthwatering apple cider donuts, it's helpful to have a few key kitchen gadgets on hand:

Digital Kitchen Scale: Accurate measurements are crucial in baking. A digital kitchen scale ensures you use the right amount of ingredients for consistent results.

Stand Mixer or Hand Mixer: While you can mix donut batter by hand, a stand mixer or hand mixer makes the process faster and more convenient, especially when working with thicker batters.

Donut Pan: A donut pan is essential for shaping and baking your donuts. Choose a quality non-stick pan for easy release.

Cooling Rack: A cooling rack allows your freshly baked donuts to cool evenly and prevents sogginess.

Pastry Brush: Use a pastry brush to apply glazes, melted butter, or oil to your donuts, ensuring a flavorful finish.

Piping Bag and Tips: For filled donuts or decorative designs, a piping bag and a variety of tips can be invaluable.

Section 2: Choosing the Right Donut Pans

When selecting a donut pan, consider the following factors:

Material: Donut pans are typically made of metal, silicone, or non-stick coated materials. Metal pans provide excellent heat conduction, while silicone pans are flexible and easy to clean. Non-stick coated pans require less greasing but should be handled with care to avoid damaging the coating.

Size: Donut pans come in various sizes, from mini donuts to standard-sized ones. Choose a size that suits your preference and the recipes you plan to make.

Shape: Traditional donut pans have a ring shape, while others feature a more decorative design, such as heart-shaped or star-shaped donuts. Select the shape that best fits your recipe or occasion.

Section 3: Mixing and Baking Techniques

Measure Ingredients Accurately: Use a digital kitchen scale to measure ingredients like flour, sugar, and spices accurately. This ensures consistent results every time you bake.

Mixing Techniques: When mixing donut batter, avoid overmixing, which can make the donuts tough. Mix just until the ingredients are combined.

Grease the Pans: Even non-stick pans benefit from a light greasing with cooking spray or butter. This helps with easy donut release.

Preheat the Oven: Always preheat your oven to the specified temperature in the recipe. This ensures even baking.

Test for Doneness: Use a toothpick or cake tester to check if the donuts are done. Insert it into a donut; if it comes out clean or with a few moist crumbs, the donuts are ready.

Cooling and Glazing: Let the donuts cool in the pan for a few minutes before transferring them to a wire rack. This prevents condensation and sogginess. When glazing, dip the donuts while they're still slightly warm for better absorption.

Chapter 12: Donut Decor and Presentation

The art of decorating and presenting your apple cider donuts can elevate them from delicious treats to visually stunning creations. In this chapter, we'll dive into the techniques for decorating donuts like a pro, explore creative donut displays, and discover how to gift-wrap donuts for special occasions.

Section 1: Decorating Donuts Like A Pro

Mastering the art of donut decoration can turn your creations into eye-catching delights:

Glazing and Toppings: Experiment with various glazes, such as chocolate, vanilla, caramel, or fruit-flavored glazes. After glazing, have fun with toppings like sprinkles, crushed nuts, mini chocolate chips, or edible flowers.

Filling Techniques: For filled donuts, use a piping bag with a filling tip to inject jam, custard, or cream into the center. Remember to dust powdered sugar on the top.

Drizzles and Swirls: Create elegant drizzles by melting chocolate or caramel and using a fork or piping bag to make decorative patterns on the donuts.

Textured Designs: Impress with textured designs by rolling your donuts in finely chopped nuts, toasted coconut, or cookie crumbs.

Section 2: Creative Donut Displays

Donuts can be served in creative and visually appealing ways:

Donut Towers: Stack donuts in tiers to form a donut tower. Use cake stands or tiered dessert stands for stability. Decorate the tower with fresh flowers or greenery for a stunning centerpiece.

Donut Wall: Create a donut wall by hanging donuts on pegs or hooks. This unique display adds a touch of whimsy to parties and events.

Donut Skewers: Thread mini donuts onto wooden skewers and arrange them in a vase or jar for a fun and portable treat.

Donut Cake: Stack donuts on top of each other to create a donut cake. Use icing to hold them together and decorate the top with glaze and toppings.

Section 3: Gift-Wrapping Donuts for Special Occasions

When you want to give the gift of donuts, presentation matters:

Donut Boxes: Place your donuts in decorative boxes lined with parchment paper. You can find specialty donut boxes or repurpose pastry boxes for this purpose.

Cellophane Bags: Slip donuts into clear cellophane bags and tie them with colorful ribbons or twine. Attach a small gift tag for a personal touch.

DIY Donut Bouquet: Create a donut bouquet by securing donuts on wooden skewers and arranging them in a vase. Add faux flowers or greenery for an elegant touch.

Personalized Labels: Design custom labels or stickers to add a personalized message or the occasion's theme to your donut packaging.

Presentation Matters: Remember that the way you present your donuts can enhance the gift-giving experience and make your treats even more special.

Chapter 13: Donut Troubleshooting

Baking perfect apple cider donuts can sometimes be a challenge, but with the right guidance, you can overcome common issues and achieve delightful results. In this chapter, we'll explore common donut baking problems, provide solutions for perfect donuts, and include a Q&A session with expert bakers to address your pressing donut-related questions.

Section 1: Common Donut Baking Problems

Donut baking problems can range from texture issues to flavor concerns. Here are some common challenges you might encounter:

Donuts are Too Dense: If your donuts turn out dense or heavy, it could be due to overmixing the batter. Overmixing can lead to the formation of gluten, resulting in a tougher texture.

Donuts are Too Dry: Dry donuts can occur if you use too much flour or bake them for too long. The key is to measure ingredients accurately and watch your baking time.

Donuts Have Uneven Color: Uneven color can happen when your oven's temperature isn't consistent. Invest in an oven thermometer to ensure accurate temperatures.

Donuts are Not Rising: Donuts may fail to rise if the leavening agents (baking powder or baking soda) are old or expired. Check the freshness of your ingredients.

Section 2: Solutions for Perfect Donuts

To achieve perfect apple cider donuts, consider these solutions:

Proper Mixing: Mix your donut batter until just combined to avoid overmixing. This ensures a tender texture.

Precise Measuring: Use a digital kitchen scale to measure ingredients accurately, especially flour. This helps maintain the right balance of dry and wet ingredients.

Temperature Control: Invest in an oven thermometer to verify that your oven maintains the correct temperature. Position your donuts in the center of the oven for even baking.

Fry at the Right Temperature: If frying, use a candy thermometer to maintain the oil temperature between 350°F to 375°F (175°C to 190°C). Too hot or too cold oil can affect donut texture.

Section 3: Q&A with Expert Bakers

In this section, we reached out to expert bakers to answer your frequently asked questions about donut baking. Here are a few examples:

Q1: Can I substitute ingredients in donut recipes?

Expert Answer: While some substitutions are possible, it's crucial to maintain the balance of wet and dry ingredients. Substituting flour types, sweeteners, or fats can alter the texture and flavor of your donuts.

Q2: How do I make gluten-free or vegan donuts?

Expert Answer: Gluten-free donuts can be made using a gluten-free flour blend, and vegan donuts can use plant-based milk and egg substitutes. Experiment with various options and adjust the recipe accordingly.

Q3: Why are my donuts oily after frying?

Expert Answer: Oily donuts can result from insufficiently hot oil or overcrowding the frying pan. Ensure the oil is at the correct temperature and fry donuts in small batches.

Chapter 14: Donut-Related Fun for Kids

Donuts are not just delicious treats; they can also be a source of fun and creativity for kids. In this chapter, we'll explore donut-themed crafts and activities, enjoy a special apple cider donut Storytime, and whip up kid-friendly donut recipes that little chefs can help create.

Section 1: Donut-Themed Crafts and Activities

Keep kids entertained with donut-themed crafts and activities:

Donut Decorating Station: Set up a decorating station with plain donuts, bowls of various colored icing, and an assortment of sprinkles, candies, and toppings. Let kids create their own edible masterpieces.

Donut Art Project: Provide paper plates, markers, and stickers for kids to create their own paper donuts. They can draw their favorite toppings and decorations.

Donut Memory Game: Create a memory game with pictures of different types of donuts on cards. Kids can take turns flipping cards to find matching pairs.

Donut Scavenger Hunt: Hide small donut toys or pictures around the house or yard, and provide clues or a treasure map for kids to find them.

Section 2: Apple Cider Donut Storytime

Gather the kids for a cozy apple cider donut Storytime. Read a classic or new children's book that features donuts or fall-themed stories. Consider titles like "If You Give a Dog a Donut" by Laura Numeroff or "The Great Doughnut Parade" by Rebecca Bond. Serve apple cider and donuts as a special treat while you read.

Section 3: Kid-Friendly Donut Recipes

Get kids involved in the kitchen with these simple and tasty donut recipes:

Mini Donut Hole Pops:
Ingredients:

- Mini apple cider donut holes
- Lollipop sticks
- Melted chocolate or icing for dipping
- Assorted sprinkles and toppings

Instructions:

1. Insert a lollipop stick into each mini donut hole.
2. Dip the donut holes into melted chocolate or icing, then decorate with sprinkles or toppings.
3. Let the kids get creative with their designs.

Donut Fruit Kabobs:
Ingredients:

- Sliced apples or bananas
- Mini apple cider donuts
- Wooden skewers

Instructions:

1. Assemble the fruit and mini donuts on wooden skewers, alternating between fruit slices and donuts.
2. Serve as a fun and nutritious snack.

No-Bake Donut Pops:
Ingredients:

- Mini apple cider donuts
- Melted chocolate
- Assorted sprinkles and toppings
- Lollipop sticks

Instructions:

1. Insert a lollipop stick into each mini donut.
2. Dip the donuts into melted chocolate, then decorate with sprinkles and toppings.
3. Allow the chocolate to set before enjoying.

Chapter 15: Donut Fundamentals

To become a donut-making expert, it's essential to understand the fundamentals of donut ingredients, mixing and proofing techniques, and a bit of donut history and trivia. In this chapter, we'll dive into these key aspects of making the perfect apple cider donuts.

Section 1: Understanding Donut Ingredients

To create delicious donuts, it's important to know the role of key ingredients:

Flour: Flour provides structure and texture. All-purpose flour is commonly used, but you can experiment with other flours like cake flour for lighter donuts.

Leavening Agents: Baking powder and/or baking soda provide the rise and fluffiness in donuts. Ensure they are fresh for optimal results.

Sugar: Sugar adds sweetness and moisture to donuts. Granulated sugar is the standard, but brown sugar or other sweeteners can be used for unique flavors.

Fats: Fats like butter or oil contribute to the tenderness and flavor of donuts. Experiment with different fats for varied tastes.

Liquid: Liquid ingredients, such as milk, buttermilk, or apple cider, provide moisture and flavor. Apple cider is a key ingredient for apple cider donuts, imparting a distinct taste.

Section 2: Mixing, Proofing, and Frying Techniques

Mixing: When mixing donut batter, avoid overmixing, which can lead to tough donuts. Mix just until the ingredients are combined.

Proofing: Proofing is the process of letting the donut dough rise before frying or baking. It allows the yeast to ferment, giving donuts their airy texture. Follow the proofing times specified in your recipe.

Frying: Frying is the traditional method for making donuts. Use a deep fryer or a heavy-bottomed pot with enough oil for donuts to float freely. Maintain the oil temperature to ensure even cooking.

Baking: Baking donuts is a healthier alternative to frying. Use a donut pan and preheat the oven to the specified temperature in your recipe. Baked donuts are typically less greasy than their fried counterparts.

Section 3: Donut History and Trivia

Explore the fascinating history and trivia surrounding donuts:

Origins: Donuts have a rich history that can be traced back to ancient civilizations. They evolved from simple fried dough to the delicious treats we know today.

National Donut Day: National Donut Day is celebrated on the first Friday of June in the United States. It was established to honor the "Donut Lassies," female Salvation Army volunteers who provided donuts to soldiers during World War I.

Donut Variations: Donuts come in many forms, including yeast-raised, cake-style, filled, glazed, and more. Each culture has its own take on these beloved treats.

Fun Facts: Discover interesting donut facts, such as the world's largest donut ever made, the most expensive donut, and the donut-related world records.

Chapter 16: Donut Parties and Events

Donuts have a unique way of bringing joy to gatherings and celebrations. In this chapter, we'll explore the world of donut parties and events, including hosting a donut tasting party, organizing donut-making workshops, and adding a delightful touch to birthdays and weddings with donut-themed celebrations.

Section 1: Hosting a Donut Tasting Party

Donut tasting parties are a delightful way to savor a variety of flavors and styles:

Donut Selection: Curate a diverse selection of donuts, including classics like glazed and chocolate, as well as unique flavors like apple cider, maple bacon, and fruit-filled varieties.

Toppings and Glazes: Set up a toppings bar with options like sprinkles, crushed nuts, flavored glazes, and whipped cream for guests to customize their donuts.

Beverages: Complement the donuts with coffee, tea, milk, or even cider for a cozy pairing.

Decorations: Create a festive atmosphere with donut-themed decorations, such as donut-shaped balloons and tableware.

Donut Scorecards: Provide scorecards for guests to rate their favorite donuts, and crown the "Donut King" or "Donut Queen."

Section 2: Donut-Making Workshops

Donut-making workshops are an interactive and educational way to engage with donut enthusiasts:

Hands-On Experience: Set up workstations with ingredients and equipment for participants to make their own donuts from scratch.

Expert Guidance: Invite a professional baker to provide guidance and tips during the workshop.

Variety of Flavors: Offer a range of donut recipes for participants to choose from, ensuring there's something for everyone.

Take-Home Treats: At the end of the workshop, participants can take home their freshly made donuts as a sweet souvenir.

Section 3: Donut-Themed Birthdays and Weddings

Donuts can add a fun and delicious twist to birthday parties and weddings:

Donut Bar at Birthdays: Set up a donut bar with assorted donuts and toppings for guests to enjoy. For birthdays, consider a donut cake as the centerpiece.

Wedding Donut Wall: Replace the traditional wedding cake with a donut wall or tower. It's a visually stunning and interactive way for guests to savor donuts.

Favor Ideas: Send guests home with donut-themed party favors, such as mini donut bags, donut-shaped cookies, or personalized donut boxes.

Donut Decor: Incorporate donut-themed decorations, such as donut-shaped table centerpieces, donut garlands, or donut-inspired wedding invitations.

Donut Dessert Stations: In addition to the wedding cake, offer a donut dessert station with a variety of donuts and accompaniments.

Chapter 17: Donut Merchandise and Collectibles

Donuts have a special place in the hearts of many, and their charm extends beyond the kitchen. In this chapter, we'll explore the world of donut merchandise and collectibles, from vintage donut memorabilia to donut-themed clothing and accessories. We'll also guide you on where to find unique donut items to satisfy your love for these delightful treats.

Section 1: Collecting Vintage Donut Memorabilia

Vintage donut memorabilia can be a delightful addition to your collection:

Donut Signs and Advertisements: Seek out vintage donut shop signs, posters, and advertisements from past eras, featuring charming graphics and typography.

Donut Tins and Boxes: Vintage donut tins and boxes often display colorful and nostalgic designs that can evoke a sense of nostalgia.

Donut Shopware: Collect vintage coffee cups, saucers, and plates from old donut shops that have distinctive branding.

Advertising Collectibles: Look for collectibles like matchbooks, menus, and matchbox covers from historical donut establishments.

Section 2: Donut Clothing and Accessories

Express your love for donuts with stylish clothing and accessories:

Donut-Themed Apparel: Find t-shirts, sweaters, and pajamas featuring donut designs, from classic glazed to quirky, colorful creations.

Donut Accessories: Explore a world of donut-themed accessories, including socks, hats, and scarves adorned with donut patterns.

Donut Jewelry: Wear your passion for donuts with pride by choosing donut-themed jewelry, such as earrings, necklaces, and pins.

Donut Pajamas: Snuggle up in cozy donut-themed pajamas that celebrate your favorite treat.

Section 3: Where to Find Unique Donut Items

Discover where to find one-of-a-kind donut merchandise:

Local Flea Markets: Explore flea markets and antique shops in your area for vintage donut memorabilia.

Online Marketplaces: Websites like Etsy and eBay often have a wide range of vintage and handmade donut items.

Specialty Stores: Check out specialty stores that focus on food-themed merchandise. These stores often carry unique donut-related items.

Donut Festivals and Events: Attend donut festivals and events, where you can find vendors selling donut-inspired merchandise and collectibles.

Custom Creations: Consider commissioning custom-made donut artwork or merchandise from artists and crafters who specialize in food-themed items.

Chapter 18: Community and Charity Involvement

Donuts have a special way of bringing people together for a good cause. In this chapter, we'll explore various ways you can use donuts to make a positive impact on your community and get involved in charitable endeavors. Discover "Donuts for a Cause," creative donut fundraising ideas, and volunteer opportunities that center around these delightful treats.

Section 1: Donuts for a Cause

Consider using donuts as a means to support important causes:

Charity Donut Sales: Partner with local bakeries or host your own bake sale, where all proceeds from donut sales go to a charitable organization or cause.

Donut Drives: Organize a donut drive, encouraging community members to donate boxes of donuts to local shelters, hospitals, or charities.

Donut Giveaways: Spread joy by giving away free donuts to essential workers, first responders, or those in need.

Section 2: Donut Fundraising Ideas

Donuts can be a creative way to raise funds for charitable projects:

Donut Run/Walk: Host a charity run or walk event with a donut twist. Participants can stop at stations to enjoy donuts, and the entry fees support a cause.

Donut Decorating Contest: Organize a donut decorating contest where participants pay an entry fee to decorate and showcase their donut creations. Judges or attendees can vote on the best designs.

Donut Auction: Hold a donut auction where local bakers or community members donate unique donuts for bidding. The funds raised can benefit a charitable organization.

Section 3: Donut Volunteer Opportunities

Volunteer your time and skills to make a difference through donuts:

Donut-Making Workshops: Offer donut-making workshops to teach community members how to create their own donuts. Donate the proceeds or the donuts to a charity of your choice.

Donut Delivery:* Volunteer to deliver donuts to senior centers, hospitals, or shelters to brighten the day of those in need.

Donut Events for Nonprofits:* Collaborate with nonprofit organizations to host donut-themed events or fundraisers that support their causes.

Donut-Related Fundraisers:* Volunteer your baking skills to create and sell donuts at fundraising events or bake sales for local charities.

Chapter 19: Donut Photography and Social Media

Donuts are not only a delight to eat but also a feast for the eyes. In this chapter, we'll explore the art of capturing perfect donut shots, building an Instagram-worthy donut feed, and mastering the art of food styling for donuts to make your delicious creations shine on social media.

Section 1: Capturing Perfect Donut Shots

Learn the techniques to capture the essence of your donuts through photography:

Lighting: Natural light is your best friend when photographing donuts. Position them near a window or in a well-lit area for soft, flattering light.

Composition: Experiment with different angles and compositions. Try overhead shots, close-ups of toppings, or capturing a hand reaching for a donut.

Backgrounds: Choose a clean and simple background to make your donuts stand out. A neutral backdrop or wooden surface often works well.

Props and Garnishes: Enhance your donut photos with complementary props like coffee cups, fresh fruit, or colorful napkins. Sprinkle some powdered sugar or toppings for extra visual appeal.

Section 2: Building an Instagram-Worthy Donut Feed

Create an Instagram feed that's dedicated to your love for donuts:

Consistent Aesthetic: Develop a consistent visual style for your donut photos. Whether it's bright and colorful or moody and rustic, stick to a theme.

Engagement: Interact with your followers by responding to comments and engaging with their content. Building a community around your donut feed can be rewarding.

Hashtags: Use relevant hashtags like #DonutLover, #FoodPhotography, or #HomemadeDonuts to reach a wider audience.

Scheduled Posts: Plan and schedule your posts to maintain a regular and engaging presence on Instagram.

Section 3: The Art of Food Styling for Donuts

Food styling is the key to making your donuts look irresistible:

Freshness: Ensure your donuts are fresh and visually appealing. For example, freshly glazed donuts glisten beautifully.

Color Palette: Choose a color palette that complements your donuts. Consider the colors of the glaze, toppings, and background.

Texture:* Add texture and depth to your photos by using props like wooden boards, textured fabrics, or vintage utensils.

Balance and Proportion: Pay attention to the balance and proportion of elements in your photo. The donut should be the star, but the background and props should enhance the composition.

Chapter 20: Conclusion

As we reach the end of this delectable journey through the world of apple cider donuts, it's time to reflect on the joy these treats bring and the many ways you can share them with others. In this concluding chapter, we'll celebrate the joy of sharing apple cider donuts, provide guidance on where your donut journey can continue, and extend our heartfelt acknowledgments and credits.

Section 1: The Joy of Sharing Apple Cider Donuts

Apple cider donuts are more than just a sweet treat; they're a source of joy and connection. They bring smiles to faces, evoke fond memories of autumn, and create moments of warmth and togetherness. The act of sharing donuts, whether with family, friends, or your community, is a simple yet powerful way to spread happiness.

Remember that donuts can be a symbol of celebration, comfort, and generosity. Whether you're hosting a donut party, participating in charity endeavors, or simply surprising a loved one with a freshly baked batch, the act of sharing donuts is an expression of love and care.

Section 2: Your Donut Journey Continues

Your journey with apple cider donuts doesn't have to end here. There are endless possibilities for exploring new flavors, techniques, and experiences related to these delightful treats. Consider the following ways to continue your donut adventure:

Experiment with New Flavors: Try experimenting with different flavor combinations, glazes, and toppings to create your own signature donut recipes.

Visit Local Donut Shops: Explore your local area for donut shops and bakeries that offer unique and seasonal donut creations. You may discover new favorites.

Connect with Donut Enthusiasts:* Join online communities and social media groups dedicated to donut lovers. Share your experiences, recipes, and photos with fellow enthusiasts.

Host Donut-Themed Events: Continue hosting donut-themed events, whether it's a donut tasting party, a donut-making workshop, or a charitable donut fundraiser.

Section 3: Acknowledgments and Credits

We extend our heartfelt thanks to everyone who contributed to this cookbook. From the talented bakers who shared their recipes to the creative photographers and stylists who captured the mouthwatering images, this project wouldn't have been possible without your passion and expertise.

We'd also like to express our gratitude to the donut enthusiasts, food bloggers, and home cooks who have celebrated the joy of apple cider donuts and inspired others to embark on their own donut journeys.

Lastly, a special thank you to our readers. We hope this cookbook has brought you joy, inspiration, and a deeper appreciation for the wonderful world of apple cider donuts.